Made and Remade

Made and Remade

Poems by Ellen Roberts Young

WordTech Editions

© 2014 by Ellen Roberts Young

Published by WordTech Editions
P.O. Box 541106
Cincinnati, OH 45254-1106

ISBN: 9781625490865
LCCN: 2014939593

Poetry Editor: Kevin Walzer
Business Editor: Lori Jareo

Visit us on the web at www.wordtechweb.com

Cover art:
Wearmouth Bridge, c. 1800. Artist: Edward Blore
Source: Sunderland Public Libraries (UK)
Photo credit: Sunderland Public Libraries / Foter.com / CC BY-NC-SA

For Peter

I am grateful to the following journals for publications as listed:

"Atomic Power": *Untitled Country*
"Evolving" and "Headache": *Lantern Journal*
"Frame Work": *Common Ground*
"Location": *Sin Fronteras Journal*
"Pasts for Sale": *Slant*
"Questioners": *the Kerf*
"Resistance" *Rockhurst Review*
"Shaken": *Snail Mail*

I am indebted to Sandra Kohler, the late Wayne Crawford, and Richard Greenfield for guidance and encouragement. Members of Desert Writers and the Thursday Poetry Workshop have given helpful critique of many of these poems in process, and Susan Bagby and Joan Glickler, my writing partners, have also provided fellowship and support. Thanks to all.

Table of Contents

About William Paley
    And His *Natural Theology*..............................11
    Obsession..13

I Paley's Watch

In Praise of Paley's Art................................17
Not for Them...18
Matters of Scale.......................................19
Parson Paley's Devotion.............................20
Shared Ground..21
Song..22

II Made For This

Likeness...25
Wonderfully Made....................................26
Habit...27
Packages..28
Analogies...29
Made and Remade....................................30
Focus 31
Coach Paley Instructs His Debate Team......32
Headache..34
Made for This..35
Lost..36

III Shaken

Encounter..39
Distances: Valley Forge..............................40
The Social Order, England, 1800................42
Social Justice..43

Chiaroscuro..44
Coming to Terms...45
Atomic Power..46
Displacement...47
Shaken..48
Pasts for Sale...49

IV Evolving

Address to the Author................................53
Opposites Attract..54
Questioners..56
Evolving...57
Jeremiad...59
Exit Strategies...60
Resistance..61
Limitations..62
Deep Waters..63
Without End..64
Sacred Texts 65

V Time Past, Time Present

Frame Work..69
Enlightenment..70
The Triumph of Reason...............................71
Complications..72
Flood Stage..73
Patching the Dike..74
No Hands...75
Bondage...76
The Potentate of Time.................................77
Time Past, Time Present..............................78

VI Location

Perspectives..81
No Return, No Finn Again...............................82
Weary with Getting and Spending..................83
The World of the Text......................................84
Incomplete..85
Utility...86
What We Stand On..87
Location...88

About the Author...91

About William Paley
And His *Natural Theology*

Although I have been writing poetry for years, I have often puzzled over how poets create themed books, starting with a particular idea and working it through to a full-length volume of poems. What could keep them going in one direction long enough to complete such a project? Then I discovered William Paley.

I "met" Paley through a study of education in the nineteenth century. His *Natural Theology*, published in 1802, was a text in a Baptist college in Illinois at which my great grandfather studied seventy years later. When I discovered the book was available in the library, I seized the opportunity to experience what my great grandfather had read. Producing a biography of my great grandfather took seventeen years. This made me dubious about the possibility of maintaining momentum to complete what I came to call my "Paley project." I needn't have worried; Paley had caught me in his net.

William Paley was a Cambridge-educated English clergyman. His *Natural Theology* presents nature, particularly the human body, as evidence not merely that there is a God but that this God is good, wise, and caring. The eye, the ear, the joints: each is a sufficient example, in design and practicality, of the skill of the Maker. While I soon recognized that Paley's world view was one of fixed order, incompatible with my awareness of evolution and change, his delight in all levels of creation was contagious.

The watch with which Paley begins his discussion is a controlling metaphor: as a watch must have had a maker, so the forms of nature must have been designed. I was well along in the project before I realized that Paley's interest in the watch has nothing to do with time, that omnipresent and powerful feature of modern life. Paley is drawn to and impressed by all manner of mechanics, of which the watch is just one example. He equally admires mills, telescopes, the new iron bridge he sees over the Wear River, and other human inventions, especially those in which he finds a parallel to some natural form.

Paley's language is rich and flowing. His broad reach provides a view of the science and culture of his time. By its very fullness, his text leads the contemporary reader to ponder how much has changed in the 200 years since his *Natural Theology* was published.

Page references for quotations from Paley's text refer to the Oxford World's Classics edition of *Natural Theology* (2006). Italics in these passages are in the text.

Obsession

for Polly

I'm fixed on this book
like a three-year-old on trucks,
a five-year-old on dinosaurs. You could
make it my motif, were I young
enough for birthday parties.

Language to sift and savor
artfully, skillfully portrays
a world of fixed order, art
and skilled contrivance.
This balance
              wavers as I wonder
at that world's collapse in
swings, cycles, evolving
life, shifting earth.

Mechanistic views dissolve in
reality's wash and rub. I
turn and read again for fragments,
museum quality gems of evidence
for a long dead argument, a fresh fix
of fine writing, proceeding
from a fine mind.

I

Paley's Watch

In crossing a heath . . . . suppose I had found a *watch* upon the ground, ...

This mechanism being observed— it requires indeed an examination of the instrument, and perhaps some previous knowledge of the subject, to perceive and understand it; but being once, as we have said, observed and understood, the inference we think is inevitable, that the watch must have had a maker — that there must have existed, at some time and at some place or other, an artificer or artificers who formed it for the purpose which we find it actually to answer, who comprehended its construction and designed its use.

Natural Theology, 7-8

In Praise of Paley's Art

His sentences unroll at length,
    at leisure, confident, equally dismissive
        of atoms and atheism, unpressured,
            never strident against opponents
                each and all unworthy.

Wonder won't tangle his tongue,
    nor a question he can't answer fester
        into doubt. His ordered
            world and spacious language
                have room for both.

As light slides into the eye
    his words penetrate the mind gently,
        by rhythm, resonance and sense
            soothe, cajole, comforting as
                a well constructed chair.

Not for Them

William Paley walks past a
mill. Admiring its mechanism
he thinks of God's making.
How to explain this? He sets
out an image, a watch among
weeds and wildflowers,

speaks to his fellow
believers, more celebration
than argument, digresses in
elaborate sentences to block
objections, counter claims
that make them anxious.

Skeptics lean in to listen,
eavesdroppers picking up
fragments, suppose his
conclusions meant for them,
withdraw unpersuaded.
They've missed the core.

Paley's reason supports
faith's cathedral for
those within, neither
its floor nor foundation,
graceful and visible
as Gothic flying buttresses

Matters of Scale

With Uranus found, the solar system seemed
complete, a sacred seven planets, wavering
orbits explained as God's hand, tinkering.

If earth is a watch, too well designed
to need constant adjustment, the planets
travel in space bigger than a grandfather

clock. Leaving his image on the ground,
the writer describes "a will that restrains
and circumscribes" the heavenly bodies,

recommends astronomy to raise
thoughts to the sublime, cannot
imagine sending a man to the moon.

Immensity interests him less than the
minute: his God a deity of the details.

Parson Paley's Devotion

". . . to almost all the bones belong *joints*; and in these . . .are seen both contrivance and contriving wisdom."
Natural Theology, 62

"Contriving" is his word
of praise, as he observes all
that is wonderfully made:
eye and ear, hip socket, knee
hinge. For him, faith and science
ride a tandem bicycle past
mill works whose mechanical arms
proclaim God's greatness by imitation.

Certain that science would solve
remaining puzzles—why blood
needs lungs, what drives
digestion—and thus confirm
the fixed and proper order of
all the body's parts, Paley
could stomach no alternatives.

But if we swung at the knee
and only bent at hip, would it
be so bad? Crops could still
be picked, laundry hung,
and we could dance all night.

Shared Ground

Walking among new-born
flies, aphids, all nature
to feed his wonder, the parson
loses regrets (the bishop's ring
never bestowed) finds comfort
in common creaturehood.

He's at home wherever
he walks, while I, creature
of foggy hills, green valleys,
walk on alien land where
nothing of profit's produced,
nothing is wasted.

A jackrabbit feeds on
freeze-battered prickly pear,
bolts at my approach,
happy in his speed, doing
what he's made for.

If the universe has a maker
is it made less lonely?
My legs being made for walking,
their motion settles my spirit.

Song

A standard how-I-met-my-lover tale:
a side trip I had not planned to take.

I stepped aside to examine this text
and got lost in the arms of his language.

Why did no siren sound? Who disconnected
the alarm on the gate to the library stacks?

Frost's road, woods, once so beguiling, chill
me now. Warm me with your summer walks,

their music of teeming insects: comfort
me with the sweet cider of your debate.

II

Made For This

I know no better method of introducing so large a subject, than that of comparing a single thing with a single thing; an eye, for example, with a telescope. As far as the examination of the instrument goes, there is precisely the same proof that the eye was made for vision, as there is that the telescope was made for assisting it.

Natural Theology, 16

Likeness

This drop-front desk's my parsonage
 parlor, where visitors come to appeal
for aid, though not in person. We

are kin, Canon Paley, though
years apart. We share one language,
though it is altered. Outdoors,

we hear soft nature, insects' buzz,
skittering quail, more clearly than
cacophonous cities far from our doors.

I claim kinship in the discipline you
take for granted, which I too acquired
in this disjointed era. Though you

would see difference, we both delight
in the draw of the work, and, I hope, in
diligence to complete it.

Wonderfully Made

Eye and ear,
exquisite in their
contrivance,
delights of design.

We see as directed,
focus filtered by
an inner camera, miss
subleties in shadow.

We hear what is new,
siren, barking dog,
the irregularity
of an old fan.

What I hear, see
defines a world for
this body to dwell in,
a home in the cosmos.

Who's watching,
who's listening? Who
is filling the gaps
in what I see, hear?

Habit

"I have sometimes wondered why
we are not struck . . . "
Natural Theology, 80

Alert to the ordinary, caught
by wonder at small creatures,
hidden muscles, as thumb or
toe is wondrous to an
infant, he has no
mantra, no method
to teach this habit of
attention, wonders at
the lack of wonder
in those who cannot stop
to look, who only admire
the new, the bold, sharply
chiseled lines, contrasting
colors that shout most
loudly in the constant press
of seen and sensed that
batters them until
like overbeaten dough
they lose their power
to rise to admiration, to
wonder at the marvels of
the bodies they inhabit.

Packages

"The brain is a nest, the eye
is a tiny architecture;"
      Richard Greenfield, *Tracer*, 34

The brain works in hiding, mechanism
encased, wrapped like a gift.

The biggest Christmas box contains another
    and another and another,
down to a very small case,
a plastic airplane,
      symbol
of a trip too big to wrap.
         Bring from
your travel a set of Russian dolls, nested
    one inside the other,
the littlest a scant design.

The eye's tiny ring
    of muscles and tendons is precise,
efficient as a geodesic dome.

The architect's elegant portal
works long hours
      drawing in scraps of light
to feed my wriggly nestlings
wrapped in makeshift walls:
    fortune cookie papers
       braided through bent twigs.

Analogies

Treasured image: curved back
of a worker bent in concentration,
watchmaker with tiny tools,

magnifying eyepiece,
or potter with clay-covered hands:
each has a skill prized in its time.

When human minds are
compared to computers, no one calls
God a computer nerd, and though

bodies are treated like machines,
repaired, regulated, no one says,
"We are watches."

We break, are mended
like serviceable jars, more kin to
vulnerable clay than clipped metal.

Paul wrote "earthen
vessels" and it stuck.

Made and Remade

"We see nothing similar to this contraction
in any machine which we can make . . ."
                              Natural Theology, 47

Some mysterious substance
whether "fluid, gaseous, elastic, electric
         or none of these" swells the muscle's
center to contract the tendons, be it
by will or "involuntary irritation."

Cause unknown, effect perceived.

The writing hand: joint activity, adjusted tendons
         of several muscles intertwined
at every stroke an "obedience of action"
whose "quickness and correctness" are so exact
it makes my penmanship, for good or ill, my own.

Lubricants more slippery than oil protect
the joints: "*how well they wear*" his italics
shout. No parallel in watch or mill to this.
                              Unperceived
(though he knows bones reknit, sprained
         tendons heal, and skin regrows under scabs)
how constant the remaking. Fluid,
throbbing, electrical, renewing itself each seven years
the body adapts, adjusts, in rhythm with
a universe ever in motion.

Focus

Paley's no Moses, his face
too close to the source, burning.
His deity, all act, too busy to sit
for a portrait, warms the writer's
back as he perceives divine
reflection in all that moves.

Michelangelo too was looking
aside, telling it slant, his figure
sparking Adam a fiction. The
ineffable in flesh, in words,
is unreal as Charlton Heston
in flowing robe. The image

tricks eye, mind to stop before
it, miss the more beyond.

Coach Paley Instructs His Debate Team
(Natural Theology, 35)

"When faults are pointed out, and
when a question is started concerning
      the skill of the artist,
          or the dexterity with which the work is executed,
              then,
    indeed,
in order to defend these qualities from accusation,

The game plan is an end run, no meeting head-to-head:

"we must be able, either
      to expose some intractableness and
          imperfection in the materials, or
point out some invincible difficulty in the execution,
      into which imperfection and difficulty
          the matter of complaint may be resolved; or,
if we cannot do this,

entangle your opponent in subordinate clauses,

"we must adduce such specimens
      of consummate art and contrivance
      proceeding from the same hand
as may convince the inquirer of the existence,
      in the case before him,
of impediments like those which we have mentioned,
      although,

imply his ignorance, impugn his knowledge

> "what from the nature of the case
> is very likely to happen,
> they be unknown or unperceived by him.

till, unable to find an opening,

> "This we must do in order to vindicate
>   the artist's skill."

he leaves the field.

Headache

Language fixes
ideas as gelatin firms
liquid, as tacks pin
manifestos to walls.
When ideas clash, terms,
modifiers do battle,
words the ammunition of
infantry and air force
alike, slogans bursting
in air. Volleys, their
number inverse to
confidence, change
atmospheric pressure
in the brain, feed
a swelling tumor
quivering like jello
where thought
should have been.
Not likely it's benign.

Made for This

Remember the day we were taught
"this desk you lean on is mostly space"

where atoms float,
their protons,   electrons,
spin, separate, combine.

What eye could not see accepted
as reality
by eager grasping minds, we leaned
just as hard, belief affecting no action,
two worldviews in suspension
from that day forward.

Space inside a church,
set apart, sanctified
to keep out wrangling,
tune our ears
toward listening,
is holy

as the space
between atoms in wood,
between stars,
anywhere call and response
reverberate, interaction
molecular or human,
matter made
for the sake of space.

Lost

"Look!" the child
wants to be seen, known,
runs to grandparent as to a cliff
he doesn't know is undercut,
fearless.

As I learned
to count, watcher turned
scorekeeper.
I began to study
the complexities of frowns.

I search the lost
and found box for the trust I dropped
in my rush to class, a straight A student
more anxious about the test
than any slacker.

Tall missiles shadowed
my school days.
Was there
less to fear
before the atom split?

I yearn for the assurance of one who,
in an era of frequent epidemics,
raids, overturned coaches, reads
nature's facts as evidence
of benevolent creation.

III

Shaken

Again, there are strong intelligible reasons, why there should exist in human society great disparity of wealth and station. Not only as these things are acquired in different degrees, but at the first setting out of life. In order, for instance, to answer the various demands of civil life, there ought to be amongst the members of every civil society a diversity of education, which can only belong to an original diversity of circumstances.

Natural Theology, 268

Encounter

An intuitive at odds with rules, the social order, the self that order has invaded, colonized, the self corrupted by conformity, wants only to leave the mind for sensation, to see, smell, hear, walks out in nature, meets there a parson, marvels at the man's delight as he describes small things, absorbs his pleasure in the small, believing this will lead to larger matters, begins a wider conversation as they see the flowers and hear the insects of the field, finds the parson is an organization man of a time when church and state were the only corporations, marvels again that they have so much in common in the little, yet so little in the large, walks back into mind refreshed by this curious new friendship.

Distances: Valley Forge

I park in a back lot to walk a
four-mile loop in the clear air,
natural landscape the Park service
mows, now one section, now
another, to keep woods out, retain
an image of then, after cutting for
huts and fires, parade ground
where deer now drill, pacing,
peering, where kites fly.

Paley and Washington, two
pragmatic Anglicans on two sides
of the Atlantic, believed they shared
one culture. Paley championed
order, crafted his argument into a
sturdy crenellated tower, no
earthen redoubt, defense of
Washington's ragtag army, no
low log hut to house the army
as they fought for a *novus ordo*.

I've peered into those huts, read
plaques, brought children to picnic,
climb cannons. Washington's
war unleashed forces
neither he nor Paley could
imagine, including school systems
where Paley would be studied,
Washington idolized, by students who
could see no difference between them,
wise men from an ever receding past.

The Social Order, England, 1800

"How should birds know that their eggs
contain their young?"
Natural Theology, 161.

The hen does not comprehend
the egg. Untutored mothers
produce offspring: mothers

denied an education, harried,
hurried as frightened chickens,
mothers of mill workers

who can do no more than
reproduce mill workers.
Unequal opportunities

set by birth, the scholar
accepts this structure as
fixed, nature's balance.

Mendel's cross-pollinated peas,
revealing nature's propensity
for change, are decades away.

Social Justice

Paley never said society
should run like a watch, nor
that it operates as God intended,
efficient as a well-oiled mill, yet
he wanted even revolution to
be rational, restrained: no mobs
dragging out Tory sympathizers,
no armies beating back
impoverished protestors.

I stand at the Federal Building,
restrained by fear, as rational
friends, frustrated by the tick,
tick, tick of same old, same
old injustices, lie across doorways.
Their calculated choice includes
awareness that effects are often
not proportionate to causes,
anything can happen.

Chiaroscuro

We see the middle ages as dim, grim,
nights always long, superstition-dulled
days briefly lightened by boisterous
cheer as Bruegel's peasants
danced in muddy streets.

As if the skies had brightened after
Gutenberg, contrasts sharpened like
a crisp Dürer engraving as trim lines
of argument by Bacon, Newton,
Linnaeus codified nature's laws.

And all was clear until Stephenson's
engine spawned coal-eating
furnaces, factory smoke. As skies
grew dark again, science turned to
invisibles: germs, electric currents.

Seeing focused on fragments:
Cezanne's boxes, Picasso's faces.
As we grope toward an unseen
future, what guides us now is loose,
tangled as Pollock's strings.

Coming to Terms

He's no specialist of any
kind, no botanist nor
astronomer, not even a
theologian, with terms,
categories, qualifiers
unique to his field.

His enthusiasm spans
anatomy and astronomy,
insects, birds, iron bridges,
helium balloons, and all
the fluids and forces he
cannot explain. They won't

be explained until scholarly
fields branch like unpruned
tomato vines, forget their
common root, produce
no more instructive apples
all can understand.

Chemist, physicist
and biologist narrow
their focus to push their
projects further, farther
apart, terms bearing fruit
as separate languages.

Atomic Power

> " . . . the antiquated system of atoms . . ."
> *Natural Theology*, 222

Curanderas have no use for smallest particles,
know plants' properties vary by the earth,

water, wind in which they grow. Chemists
diagram atoms linked in hexagons,

isolating compounds from plants that heal,
won't replicate environments. It's enough

to synthesize the complex molecule,
as if its host were irrelevant, as if bodies

were only stacks of atoms, not
columns of energy in constant interplay.

Displacement

Did Paley's God, observing
through a watchmaker's lens,
neglect free agency's side effects?
Immigrants seek work, emigrants
escape catastrophe, all creatures
move into others' space,
squirrels at bird feeders,
bears in campgrounds.

Always in motion, our race
stretched, flexed, made
such a run it seems we have
outpaced plans of a deity
whose contrivances for future use
could only reach so far, from
lungs in the fetus to
mother's milk to mature teeth.

From McCormick's reaper to Ford's
assembly line to Jobs' Apple
invention builds, cascades, creates
a mass of humanity dissatisfied,
disoriented as coyotes
circling a new development.

Shaken

As a child in earthquake country
I knew the earth could shift
yet walked with confidence,
assured the fault did not lie
under the house.

When political tremors spilled
boxes into Boston harbor, an
Englishman's table, set with tea
from Ceylon or India, fresh milk,
Caribbean sugar, did not tip.

New voices cried from far countries,
colonies. In science, physics and
chemistry undermined foundations.
Causes widened like the Atlantic,
deepened into canyons.

Upheavals everywhere, I learn no
house is safe. Leave silver locked
up, set teapots on tray tables ready
to be folded at the first
faint rumble.

Pasts for Sale

Three purple napkins, a long green tablecloth,
silver gone black. A faint mildew odor
drifts from basement-stored books. We
bump elbows, focused on Santas and
skeletons, picture frames, figurines, gathering
up items useful and useless to support the cause
this rummage sale benefits.

Pieces are all we have of the past, the smaller
available for taking as if spread on tables:
discolored engravings, chipped cups,
tokens for travel on a train. The larger,
popular items are in the antiques market,
among Queen Anne and Shaker chairs:
Washington at the Delaware, Franklin's kite
(the key lost), Jefferson's wall of separation.
Changing hands again and again, they've been
cleaned, remounted, tinted by each purveyor
to suit each buyer.

I pick out old account books, painted plates,
grandfather stories, printed pages.
Believing I am true to my modest
acquisitions, I mount sections of text,
cut from their context, in contemporary
frames to furnish my study.

IV

Evolving

Upon the whole; after all the struggles of a reluctant philosophy the necessary resort is to a Deity. The marks of *design* are too strong to be got over. Design must have had a designer. The designer must have been a person. That person is God.
Natural Theology, 229

Address to the Author

Schooled like you to the linear,
accepting each text as a
false fronted building without
side entrance or back alley,
I would read voraciously,
a bookworm. Have you
noticed worms, unlike
caterpillars, don't get fat?

Nature no she, the only females
in your world are mindless hens,
ignorant sparrows. As a student
I'd not have noticed this absence.
I'm pleased to be meeting you
in maturity, to see the craft in
your statements, no mere
conveyors of data as you delight
in, meditate on mechanism.

I'll not mistake this text for
a second scripture, a Talmud
or Mishnah, nor a sure defense
of one specific reading of creation,
yet your certainty satisfies my
taste like green chili on beef
as I burrow into your book.

Opposites Attract

God dismissers, needing
no meddling Him, toss
words at the devout, who
counter with their own
in endless debate.

Most of us ignore
their argument, limit
our opinions to the latest
celebrity in jail or whether
Pluto is a planet, too busy
to ponder issues news
reporters will not ask about.

I was busy checking off
tasks I thought important,
when William Paley entered.
Philosopher-pastor, no
wordslinger, phrase thrower,
he lays out his propositions
as a thick, inviting carpet.

I won't say Paley's right, lest
you think I speak of science,
yet he's not wrong to marvel
at the world, its workings.

His language carries me
beyond argument, his or
mine or theirs, beyond
odorless debate, onto
a sweet-smelling meadow,
the sacred.

Questioners

That watch, now archaic
artifact: he doesn't ask how
it got there. We do, cued in
that everything has a past,
nothing springs *ex nihilo*
from one pair of skilled hands.

Teasing out clues where evidence
is scant we may be wrong:
Mesa Verde's abandonment,
declared "result of war"
in the forties, was blamed on
climate change in the eighties.

Study of primates, DNA,
has pushed God into a corner –
the God shaped, limited by
human interpretation. Abandon
that image: we're no more
distanced from the divine

than my refusal
to wear a watch
releases me from time.

Evolving

Picture the Sistine deity
sparking Adam, then
sitting back to
observe each intricate
eye and limb
formed, planted. From
a glowing throne this God
watches flowers grow, bees
make honey, humans
discover its sweetness,
the snake . . . .

Wars and rumors of war
slither through centuries.
England, France, Germany,
Spain hiss and strike,
the nineteenth century
dream of progress as
peace shattered
by the twentieth:
trenches, gas, air strikes.

Bitter fruit makes us no wiser.
Regimes rise and
fall hard
as Adam. War sheds its
European skin, swells
in the desert, larger,
stronger. The wall's tumble
echoes, heard
here as freedom, there
as ruin, rippling chaos.

Jeremiad

We honor Jeremiah,
prophet, doomsayer,
for constancy to his God.
Now doomsday clocks
proliferate, reset by
anxious watchmen as
claims counter claims.

Since *Silent Spring*,
doomsday's put off,
payments due on
borrowed time delayed.
Some propose cures:
"return to the land, buy
local, make it yourself."

Cries reverberate, clog
ears. The question,
"How can we get back
to where we once
belonged?" is met
with silence. Not one
of us has been there.

None of us will hear
the clocks' final chime.

Exit Strategies

Two centuries of increasing
speed, fire-fed machines
on land, in air. Too clever
to be fooled by pretty pasts,
we look forward: will there
be peace? What of those
Mayan claims for 2012?

Cosmic battle? In its
midst we find no promise,
cry to be in that number
airlifted out by divine
aid, to a broad green park
or a twelve-gated city
with everflowing river.

Faster engines, higher
flights provide no calm,
no comfort, nothing we can
grasp to steady, save us.

Resistance

Babes too young to choose the good
we put everything in our mouths.
Offered new ideas, I spit some out,
swallow some whole, no patience
for picking over the text, separating
meat from shells, testing the odor.

Untrained in culling thoughts,
we seek alternate routes, any detour
from the slow crawl to maturity,
or set up boundaries, safety bars
fixed as slats on our old cribs against
the move from true/false questions
to paragraphs, subjunctives, awkward
as learning to balance on two feet.

Drained by my efforts, I say
I'd rather sleep on the floor than
return to a crib, as if there were
no other bedrooms in this mansion
of intellect, no blended coffee, no rich
infusions to replace the milk of infancy.

Limitations

A potter may find she's got
    a bad batch of clay,
        a wheel out of balance.

The watch maker bends his metal
    too far, the spring's inadequate
        to hold the tension.

A builder discovers the stone needed
    to support his planned structure
        will not fit the space.

The poet molds, coils words as if they
    could move stone, congeal
        matter out of sound.

Creatures aspiring to create
    we forget how close we are
        to clay, metal, stone, air.

Deep Waters

The builder meant his craft, no raft
of lashed poles, no stumbling
ad hoc argument, for quiet waters,
gentle contemplation.

Its new owners bend
science to add a protective hull,
can't correct the structure,
ill-designed to carry the weight
of scriptural defense.

Paley saw no threat in new knowledge,
could not foresee how Darwinian
storms would knock out piers of
consensus, dislodge his logic.

His successors send his sloop,
a clumsily armored David, among
huge grey hulks merely inconvenienced
when a fresh blow drives
his craft's elegant sails
into their path.

Without End

Scientists drop deity with design.
The one praised as designer early
in the machine age is inadequate
to their new knowledge. Their
universe moves without a maker.

I too dislike the hands-on,
strong-arm straw man of atheist
argument, have shelved him with
childhood's wooden trains, toy trucks.

The God who appeared as master
of war in primitive Palestine, as
master mechanic in the industrial era,
has shed all labels, gone before us
into the next new age.

Sacred Texts

"To read Leviticus is to enter a foreign world."
      Michael Tassler, sermon, 2011

Gas burning in another room
warms my bare toes. I have
no need to feed the fire.

Familiar words—sabbath, peace
offering, jubilee, love your
neighbor—are sifted from Mosaic
law, its unfamiliar world of
herds and sacrifice, cereal
offerings, clean and unclean, rules
circumscribing an unruly people
to make them holy, servants of their God.

I open *Natural Theology*
thinking I know this language, yet
something's lost in translation when
Paley calls all creatures happy:
from insect to human, happy as Jefferson
meant it, rightly placed. Anglican in
ordered England, this writer saw no
need to pursue, grasp at such happiness.

Leviticus' authors knew better. Order's a
goal, impossible to sustain, must be
regained by frequent washing,
whitened clothes, fenced by priestly
inspection, a holding against disorder
I sense only when power goes out, I
grope for candles, grab a blanket.

Practice of holiness, pursuit of happiness,
long treated as opposites are
parallel as lines of a Hebrew psalm;
holy is happy, longed for, labored for.
What sacrifice or sabbath
can set us right now the Temple's fallen,
mills moved overseas, religion and state
are at odds and no sign separates
stranger from neighbor?

I can scarcely hear migrating birds
over the furnace drone.

V

Time Past, Time Present

By inspecting the watch, . . we get a proof of contrivance . . . . But, when we see the watch *going*, we see proof of another point, viz. that there is a power somewhere and somehow or other applied to it, a power in action . . . .

Natural Theology, 217

Frame Work

When you say "face reality"
you're pointing to
an ordering you've
overlaid, a pattern you cut
the world to fit. This naming
helps, then hinders. I see,
seesaw into not seeing, still
within the arc of your compass.

North star and constellations
no longer serve. We want
a new configuration to guide
our native-born yet alien race
in a world of too many
languages we have not
learned. Every name
we utter is translation.

The sky is still a dome. Stars
pierce the smoke-darkened
ceiling of our cluttered
house, nature's balance
clumsily reshaped, its give
and take constricted by
engineers of stone and seed.

Seeing this, what image
can I find to name my grieving?

Enlightenment

Three hundred years
of seeing dark behind
and light ahead have
strained our eyes.

Hopes dashed by wars
and rumors of wars, I hear
some cry "Armageddon!"
while others grope for ancient
wisdom, find a few stones
that sparkle, sit under—
or in—aged trees.

"Everything old is
new again"—isn't that
just a riff on Ecclesiastes?
The bored preacher,
who's seen it all, wraps
his "no progress" message
in eloquence I savor.

But my zen professor says
"It's all in how you look at it."
His crystal, catching
the light, entices me.

The Triumph of Reason

Minds aflame with new learning
cleared forests superstition
claimed as haunted, squared
a sacred center with grids
of logic, knowledge.

The a and b of a syllogism,
bare statements, go
underground, root
as assumptions, until an
earthquake destroys the premises.

The shattered structure
catches fire, water damage
leaves it awash in mud.
What use a grid when you're struck
from below and above?

All your training has bent you
toward repair, replacement:
shore up foundations,
rebuild, repress the urge
to abandon these premises.

Yet you imagine a forest hut,
low to the ground, is safer, think
appeasing fretful spirits must be
easier, as you recut, trim, stack
each precise, logical block.

Complications

If fire were always a blessing, mud
never a nursery, black not clothes
for the righteous, we could
go by appearances, but when
Prometheus stole fire from heaven
evil caught in its train, brown
mud on a bride's hem.

Knowledge looked up from
stacking ideas like bricks
without straw. Desire found new
yearnings to plant in human hearts.

And both put on black tuxedos
to attend the wedding of heaven
and hell which birthed our
muddled world, where the mob
leader's kindness is proverbial,
while an ethics professor
abandons his ailing wife.

Flood Stage

Information makes no orderly advance,
can no more stay in formation than water.
Voices near and known, printed pages once
brought varied tales to our door. Now both
cross distance at a run, cascading, overflowing
banks, tumble in unscreened through
every window. Another deluge of data, an
avalanche in Mistrust Mountains, swells

the flood with brush, trash, silt, stones.
Our maps of higher ground torn, smudged,
we ponder which risk to take, to flee or stay.
Children, intent on texting, don't follow.
They've never seen that place, faint in our
memories, where Understanding Creek,
glacier fed, runs clear, makes luminous
the variegated stones that form its bed.

Patching the Dike

"A law presupposes an agent
    ... it implies a power."
        Natural Theology, 217

Law is nothing
without the one who orders it,
whose power gives it effect.

Nature
is not that power, is not
an entity, the philosopher declares.

As one who resists
those vermin terms that creep
into improper places, he speaks

with authority, that of an English
teacher in a world of slang.

No Hands

In dream, the old watch
I wear on my wrist gives
time exact but inconsistent:
ten to eight at the next glance is
8:10, "late" suddenly "very late,"
judgment I read in an instant.

Children in the after-school program
slowly count out the minute marks
on the wall clock, learning new
signs, a process I don't remember.
The precision of sixty second minutes
is not in our psyches, yet

taking my son's temperature I watch
the second hand go round twice and
again and in its circle I am comforted.
That round clock face is remnant:
these children live in a linear world,
advance without respite.

Bondage

Study of skies, feared
as idolatry, obedience to planets,
was banned by the church,
while farmers on a flattened earth
continued to plant by the moon, prayed
for rain to El or Baal or Ceres, any
god who might assist them.

Only bare numbers, base sixty,
remained of ancient science. Clocks
gained precision, slivered hours
into sixty minutes of sixty seconds
as if to conquer by division.

Unable to rule the world, clocks
control those who made them.
Minutes obscure moments: noon's
shimmer, evening's slow dimming.
Enslaved by our servants, we
are chained in the circle
of one to sixty, one to sixty.

The Potentate of Time

As CEO, I cannot allow loss
of minutes dropped by badly
calibrated clocks, seconds

split by timers racing after
ever faster miles, or precious
nanoseconds sliced, spit out

by precision machines: all
the clumsy human attempts
to alter time.

I dispatch work crews to
sweep corners and gutters, sift
bits from curbs and drains,

bring their gathered goods into
my laboratory where skilled
artisans sort, stitch, splice. My

expanding universe requires
recovery, repair, reuse
of every particle.

Time Past, Time Present

What's the time on Paley's watch?
Without hands it would still be
a watch. It's mechanism matters
to him: springs and metal, not hours,
minutes. His present so long
past, timeless in comparison
with ours, has he a gift for the now
in which we're timebound?
Precision of seconds has taken us
into space—we've seen the moon
under astronauts' feet, the earth from
distance, expanded vision enabled by
diminution: binary, bytes, microchips.

His offering disrupts the chattering
minutes of everyday life like news of
inheritance from a forgotten great uncle.
How shall it be received? I can't
live in his house: no plug for a
computer, no phone line for internet.
A distracted decorator, I survey
attractive images, small items I could
add to my already cluttered world. No,
I'll ask his executors for the stout oak
table of his attention to detail, his eye
for analogies, gift I can use to interpret
pulse and rhythm of this present.

VI

Location

The manner of it is this: the end of the rib is divided by a middle ridge into two surfaces . . . . Now this is the very contrivance which is employed in the famous iron bridge at my door at Bishop-Wearmouth . . .
Natural Theology, 59

Perspectives

Walking in this desert I can picture you at work in your study because I have also walked on cobbled streets by Independence Hall, seen portrayed the men who met there, your contemporaries. Your manse in a northern town at a river's mouth calls to mind rocky shores I've walked on, their ten foot tides; I can see you there. Yet, walking on sand I too easily picture your heath as always yellow, forget your concrete details do not become sidewalks, driveways alongside asphalt roads. You have no need to bind with cement, build on your discrete images; all point in the same direction, while my direction shifts with desert winds.

No Return, No Finn Again

Time flies? It is we
who fly, above the
surface or on it: a scurry
six feet deep in canyon
bottoms, at Sixth Ave.
and 34th Street, or
Fifteenth and Walnut.
There's nothing
commodious
about this vicus,
too frantic full,
people jammed,
in persistent
staccato, presto.

We blame railroads,
Wilbur and Orville.
It's not their fault;
increased speed
can't bring us
to an exit ramp off
time's one way street,
without a roundabout,
no recirculation,
no route back to
Howth Castle or
the new iron bridge
across the tides
at Wearmouth.

Weary with Getting and Spending

The poet stares at the sea,
wants Proteus, the shape-shifter,
for his companion, Triton's horn
for song – does that weathered
instrument still play?

His culture's cut him off
from nature, a walk on the heath
no cure for a spirit too hardened
to hear its music. His malaise
has spread. Coffee spoons
can't measure out the grandes,
ventes that fuel our enterprise.

I too have run from the mall,
stared at the bay, learned
it only reflects my anxiety,
sends up no demigod nor even
a nymph to rouse me.

As I turn from the water, will you
join me in a walk? Though
the season's short for daffodils
—or poppies—the pines
may sing some sense into us.

The World of the Text

Rereading, I discover my
error: this book on nature's forms
is no guidebook, no map: it's a fence
solid as one around a construction site,
no peepholes cut, through which
I might view the writer's world.

Words paint this wall, set on a
pedestal each chosen example,
invite me to walk around
a museum exhibit welcoming
visitors, no more a witness
to the author's time than,

in the Vatican, Laocoon and his
sons battling great snakes convey
the life of ancient Greece, though
the sculpture's careful composition
exposes civilization's anxiety.
Art, where I wished for a window.

Incomplete

In an age of reason, religion
masquerades as science—
Blavatsky's Theosophy, or
Eddy's *Science of Health*.

Logic mistakes mystery
for unknowns waiting to be
known, puzzles, problems
in a child's math book.

"Product of the Enlightenment"?
Rationalists deny the hidden
engine: emotion that fuels
their pursuit, intuition's sparks.

Cold light, not warming the ground,
produces no viable offspring,
unlike Uranus and Gaia,
grandparents of the Gods.

Utility

"where . . . it would be useless . . . no order
whatever is perceived, because it would have
been superfluous."

Natural Theology, 43

Too practical to value play
the theologian interprets lack
of order as restraint, can't
see tumbled rock,
folded strata, as excess,
a spilling over.

If stones did not break ragged
how would hominids
have developed tools? If shorelines
had simple curves, we'd lack
those inaccurate maps as sailors and
surveyors puzzled out
the new-found American coast,
its coves to shield lovers' canoes
or contraband.

Ordered shores, stone
would be useful
as flat feet: no urge
to dance, no unexpected
angle to unsettle
our assumptions.

What We Stand On

Like uneven joists below
floorboards, understanding
slants us. Stories, injunctions
of childhood underlie layered
cross pieces, the boards
of education nailed onto them.

Recognition's a matter of
shape, not substance.
Family sayings, forgotten
morals of books read young
tilt my perception. The person
before me is not a text

laid out for interpretation or
a client for five-cent analysis
by Dr. Lucy at her lemonade stand.
People can only be understood
on their own ground, and I
cannot move off mine.

Location

Among maples whose branches touched sky I reached
for ideas' edges, puzzled them into place,
a creature believing I could know
                      something of my creator.

William Paley wrote in a manse in northern England,
winters permitting long, deep thoughts. On these
premises, using his Cambridge tools,
                      he built his reputation.

His argument simple: a watch, therefore
a watchmaker. His evidence single:
an eye, an ear, a muscle,
                      any one example suffices.

I have loved such logic but I've moved
to the desert whose demanding light,
unmeasured lumens, kills
                      what sprouts after scant rain.

Away from those sheltering trees, I meet jackrabbit,
quail, who teach me strengths of survivors,
limits to my reach.
                      The sun bleaches my lines.

About the Author

Ellen Roberts Young is a member of the writing community in Las Cruces, NM., where she has lived with her husband, Peter, since 2004. Her chapbooks *Accidents* (2004) and *The Map of Longing* (2009) were published by Finishing Line Press. She is co-editor of *Sin Fronteras/Writers Without Borders Journal* and produces a monthly email list of literary events in southern New Mexico called Kery's list (keryslist@cs.com). She blogs at www.freethoughtandmetaphor.com. When not at her desk, she enjoys gardening, walking on desert trails, and sewing quilts for Project Linus.